Animal Magnetism

Animal Magnetism

At Home with Celebrities
& Their Animal Companions

Patti Denys & Mary Holmes

SMITHMARK

Half title page: Earl McDonnell
Title page: Matuschka with Liberty, Voler Wyeth

SMITHMARK books are available for bulk purchase for sales promotion and premium use. For details, write or call the manager of special sales, SMITHMARK Publishers, 115 West 18th Street, New York, NY 10011.

Produced by SMITHMARK PUBLISHERS
115 West 18th Street, New York, NY 10011.

Photography: Patti Denys and Mary Holmes
Photo Editor: William Wegman
Design: Leah S. Carlson
Editor: Kristen Schilo, Gato & Maui Productions

0-7651-9051-6

Library of Congress Catalog Card Number: 97-62147

Printed in Hong Kong

10 9 8 7 6 5 4 3 2 1

Acknowledgments

Thank you to our parents, Maurine and Sidney Denys, and Jo and Bud Holmes, who raised us in the belief that a family is incomplete without the presence of companion animals. Thanks also to all the friends who lent us support throughout the six years it took to make *Animal Magnetism* a reality, especially Bill Wegman and Christine Burgin. Special acknowledgements to our agent, Bob Markel, for helping us navigate through uncharted waters and to Kristen Schilo, our editor, who from the beginning, understood the vision of this book as if it were her very own.

Animal Magnetism would not have been possible without the extraordinary support of Maurine Denys, who babysat our companion animals so that we were free to photograph everyone else's. Many thanks to our companion animals for their patience and understanding during all the hours we spent away from them photographing others. Lastly, thanks to Linda McCartney, our role model extraordinaire. Because of her, we are both photographers and vegetarians. Her photography and animal advocacy are the ultimate inspiration behind this project.

Patti Denys

Mary Holmes

Contents

Dedication 8

Foreword by Linda McCartney 9

Introductions

   Ingrid Newkirk 10
   Jane Goodall 12

MICKEY ROONEY, Actor *16*

CAROLINE THOMPSON, Director/Screenwriter *18*

CLEVELAND AMORY, President, *The Fund for Animals* 20

JAMIE WYETH, Artist *22*

BEVERLY JOHNSON, Model *24*

BURGESS MEREDITH, Actor *26*

GRETCHEN WYLER, Broadway and Television
   Actress/Founder/President *ARK Trust, Inc.* *28*

WYLAND, Artist *30*

ROBERT PASTORELLI, Actor *32*

THE HONORABLE YVONNE BURKE,
   Supervisor, Los Angeles County *34*

TONY LA RUSSA, Manager, *St. Louis Cardinals* *36*

BEATRICE WOOD, "Mama of Dadaism" *38*

JOEL GREY, Actor *40*

RUE MCCLANAHAN, Actress/Comedienne *42*

INGRID NEWKIRK, President, *PETA* (People for
   the Ethical Treatment of Animals) *44*

LORETTA SWIT, Actress *46*

JUDY COLLINS, Singer/Musician/Author *48*

THOMAS SCHUMACHER, Executive Vice-President,
   Walt Disney Feature Animation and Walt Disney
   Theatrical Productions *50*

BOB HOPE, Comedian *52*

AUDREY FLACK, Artist *54*

TIONNE WATKINS, Singer, *TLC* *56*

SONNY BARGER, Hell's Angel *58*

KEVIN NEALON, Comedian, and LINDA NEALON *60*

VICKI LAWRENCE, Comedienne *62*

R.C. GORMAN, Artist *64*

MICHELLE PHILLIPS, Actress *66*

ELLIOTT GOULD, Actor *68*

SUE COE, Artist *70*

GREG LOUGANIS, Diver/Olympic Gold Medalist *72*

EARL HOLLIMAN, Actor/President, *Actors and
   Others for Animals* *74*

BARBARA BACH STARKEY, Actress *76*

JUDY CHICAGO, Artist *78*

LAUREN SHULER-DONNER *and* RICHARD DONNER,
   Producers/Directors *80*

ALEX PACHECO, Chairman, *PETA* *82*

MIMI ROGERS, Actress *84*

DANNY ELFMAN, Musician/Composer *86*

WILLIAM WEGMAN, Photographer *88*

GRACE SLICK, Singer, *Jefferson Airplane/Starship* *90*

SID CAESAR, Actor/Comedian *92*

SARA GILBERT, Actress *94*

ALEXANDRA DAY, Author and Illustrator, *Carl* *96*

JAMES CROMWELL, Actor *98*

ROBERT WEATHERWAX, Trainer *100*

ROBERT RAUSCHENBERG, Artist *102*

TONY CURTIS, Actor, and JILL VANDENBERG *104*

JANE GOODALL, PH.D., CBE, World-renowned
Chimpanzee Expert/Conservationist *106*

DUDLEY MOORE, Actor/Comedian/Musician *108*

MATUSCHKA, Photographer/Breast Cancer Activist *110*

MAX PERLICH, Actor *112*

MARY FRANN, Actress *114*

MONTY ROBERTS, Horse Trainer/Author,
The Man Who Listens to Horses *116*

SHERA DANESE FALK, Actress/Singer *118*

PETER VIDMAR, Gymnast/Olympic Gold Medalist *120*

RACHEL ROSENTHAL, Performance Artist *122*

ENGELBERT HUMPERDINCK, Singer, and
LOUISE DORSEY *124*

LEE STARKEY, Artist *126*

MARC DAVIS, Animator, One of Walt Disney's
"Nine Old Men" *128*

MARTINA NAVRATILOVA, Tennis Legend *130*

DAVID ELLEFSON, Musician, *Megadeth* *132*

PAUL WATSON, Captain, *Sea Shepherd*, Founder *Sea
Shepherd Conservation Society* *134*

TASHA TUDOR, Artist *136*

JOHN PAUL DE JORIA, President,
John Paul Mitchell Systems *138*

DENISE BROWN, Activist, and SEAN BROWN *140*

ALEXIS ROCKMAN, Artist *142*

CATHERINE OPIE, Artist *144*

ROY ROGERS and DALE EVANS, Actors/Singers *146*

ELLIOTT ERWITT, Photographer *148*

LINDA ELLERBEE, Producer/Journalist/Author *150*

TODD OLDHAM, Fashion Designer *152*

PATRICK MCDONNELL, Cartoonist, *Mutts* *154*

Sources 156

Credits 160

Dedication

Animal Magnetism is dedicated to the unknown millions of people and their animal companions, whose bonds are no less enduring and inspiring than those featured within these pages.

Before we began working on this book, our first official attempt at animal advocacy was helping to co-found *STAR Rescue*, an animal rescue group in San Antonio, Texas, in the mid-1980s. After years of seeing humans in the worst possible relationships with animals, we were in search of another outlet. As both of us are long-time photographers, we decided to use our skills to create something that would focus on the positive relationship between people and their companion animals. By design, we set about to gather an eclectic group of subjects, to demonstrate that this bond exists regardless of the age, sex, or occupation of the humans, and the type of companion animal.

Through *Animal Magnetism*, we honor the memory of Susie Shryrock and her three dogs Josh, Andy, and Jones. Susie, an emergency room nurse, was walking by a remote construction site with her dogs in January, 1992. After she fell and lost consciousness, her loyal and loving dogs stayed by her side all night, snuggling close to keep her warm on a night the temperature fell to 40 degrees. The following day, a helicopter rescue team sent to search for Susie was able to locate her because of her dogs' vigil.

We never got the opportunity to photograph Susie and her dogs, as she did not regain consciousness, and died a week later. It is the spirit and dedication of Susie and those like her, and the oft-mentioned unconditional love of companion animals, as so selflessly demonstrated by Josh, Andy, and Jones (who was rescued by Susie as a pup), that serve as the inspiration for *Animal Magnetism*.

By purchasing this book, you have already contributed to the welfare of animals, as a portion of *Animal Magnetism*'s profits will be contributed to PETA and to the Jane Goodall Institute. If you would like to take a further step, please consult the Sources located at the end of this book.

Foreword

This is a book of contradiction, a book about the way we are and the way we could let ourselves be.

This contradiction has puzzled and anguished me for much of my life. Hopefully, through books like this, people will see this contradiction—and when they see it—realize the ease in which we can live a better way.

The pictures in this book tell the way we are—people with their pets who share a love. That is the way we are. We all have it within us to give that love to our pet, and many of us daily show no greater love. Yet each year millions of animals that nobody loved are slaughtered and sliced up for us to eat off our plates. Isn't that a contradiction?

Isn't it crazy that we can love a cat but eat a cow? Does it make sense that we can read our children the story of *The Three Little Piggies* at bedtime, and then wake up the next morning to bacon for breakfast? Isn't it odd that we delight in looking at baby lambs playing in the fields, and then we drive home to tuck into one of them for dinner? If anyone suggested that we took any of the pets in this book and served them up for supper, there would be an outcry across the land. Little murmur marks the daily death of many animals for meals.

That is the contradiction. If we could only find it in ourselves to extend this love for our pets to all animals, then wouldn't we live in a better place? To have a love for all animals is the way that we could be. That love isn't hard to find, we already have it in us and show it to our pets. It is pictured on the face of every person in this book.

Read on and think of that. Make the connection and tell your friends. This day you could change your life to help save all life. And it only takes one thought.

love

Linda McCartney

Linda McCartney

Introduction

In the early 1980s, I traveled from the Rockies to the Florida Panhandle, and from the Golden Gate Bridge to the Chesapeake Bay, talking to people about the sorry state of our relationship with all the other animals on the face of the Earth. I was, and still am, agitating for a recognition of the wonders of even the tiniest or oddest of our fellow beings, like Bandit, (the rat on artist Sue Coe's shoulder), or Sammy (the turkey you see pictured with me on page 44).

In San Antonio, I met Patti Denys and Mary Holmes. Thanks to their hard work with *Man and Beast, Inc.*, low-cost spay/neuter operations were made possible for dogs and cats belonging to low-income families in southern Texas. Their concern for animals ensured that countless puppies and kittens would be saved from roadside desertion or from being forced to scrounge for scraps in garbage dumps. Patti and Mary were also working to stop the local city pound from using hot, unfiltered truck exhaust to choke unwanted animals to death. To combat what they saw happening around them, they founded *STAR Rescue*, a volunteer force that provided emergency services to animals who have been beaten or starved by human hands. They knew the key to ending the cycle of cruelty around them was to reach people's compassionate core and to get them to relate to animals.

Through *Animal Magnetism*, Patti and Mary have come up with another way to demonstrate how precious the bonds are between us and other-than-human beings. I only wish my dogs, Ms. Bea and Conchita, were alive to participate in this touching testimonial to the love so easily shared between species.

Ms. Bea looked something like a cross between a German Shepherd and a couch (she loathed all forms of exercise except eating). When I adopted her, she was fiercely angry at the world because her previous human had cast her aside one day as if she were no more important than a tennis racket. She distrusted my overtures, and when I reached down to stroke her head, she bit clear through my watchstrap! She died when she was about seventeen, by then a grande dame of a dog that had finally forgiven people for the many unkindnesses shown to her in puppyhood.

Conchita was one of those little, yappy Chihuahua-type dogs I used to think of as annoying—until she took over my life. When she was middle aged (but not more than six inches tall at the tips of her velvety white ears), she had been found by the roadside in a snowstorm on a bitter winter's night. A police officer unceremoniously dumped her at the county pound, where days later I discovered her bent almost in two from malnutrition, thin, and shivering out on the cold concrete floor. I picked her up just to warm her, having no intention whatsoever of taking her home, yet there she stayed in my arms almost constantly for the next nine years. How I wish I could again hear that bizarre little Chihuahua noise she would make to warn me of any impending dangers, real or imagined.

Conchita and Ms. Bea left me with wonderful memories, aside from an enormous sense of loss. Losing such loving companions caused me to reflect on how many opportunities I had to show them how much they meant to me and to make their world a little happier. *Animal Magnetism* does the same thing: it reminds us how much love there is waiting to be shared—if only we would open our eyes, our hearts, and our minds.

There is a wholeness, a connectedness, in the eyes of people who are in the company of their animal companions, a recognition that they are a part of something bigger than the narrowest definitions of our "own kind."

To recognize how complete and self-sufficient animals are in the natural world means putting an end to making sandwiches out of them, stealing their skins, and regarding them as nothing more than test tubes with tails. Thanks to Patti and Mary's work and the images in this lovely book, we are another tiny step closer to such a vision of a more compassionate world.

Ingrid Newkirk

Introduction

*A*nimal Magnetism is a beautiful and powerful book. Each photograph, taken with sensitivity and love, brings its own message; they could stand on their own. But, there is also the text; the statements and testimonies of humans who were photographed with their favorite animal companions, add a whole new dimension to the book. The two art forms together provide much food for thought.

I hate to think of a world where there would be no animals with whom to share my life, for they bring the sort of companionship that we can almost never find with members of our own species. I remember all of my animal friends. I remember the succession of cats, Pickles, Figaro, and Jaffa, rubbing against my skinny child legs, whiskers pushed back, tails carried high, backs arched. I enjoyed watching them curl up and purr in front of the fire on a cold winter's night, feeling their needling claws as the warmth of my lap transported them back to the delights of early kittenhood, when they nursed from their mothers. I also loved watching them from my window early in the morning, as they twirled and leapt, chasing dead leaves spiralling in an autumn breeze.

But for me, dogs come first. I grew up with a white bull terrier, Peggy. She was overprotective of our family as far as the postman and milkman were concerned (she never hurt them, but my parents were always having to replace their trousers!) Peggy was the perfect guardian for a small, adventurous child. Yet, the true companion of my childhood was Rusty. I met him when I was about twelve years old, and, together, we shared some ten wonderful years. There is nothing like the unconditional love of a loved dog.

I am writing this in the old red brick house in Bournemouth where I grew up. Wisky Bisky, a glorious brindled Staffordshire cross, has his head on my feet and is gently snoring, tired from our evening scramble down the cliffs to the sea (where as a child, I used to "train," for I knew not when I would finally get to Africa). Yet, if I were to say the magic word, his tiredness would be gone in a flash and he would be ready, bounding with excitement, tail waving and eyes beaming with joy and sheer love of life. Between Rusty and Wisky Bisky were Dido, a little white poodle, and Cida, a golden Shetland cross. They all had distinctive personalities, none replacing their predecessors, but arriving to help ease the ache of loss and fill the void with their own unique canine contributions to the daily toil.

Animals are utterly sympathetic to our moods—subdued when we are sad, exuberant when we share our moments of joy. It is now proven that animals can have a beneficial effect on human health. People who live with companion animals are likely to be more healthy and less depressed than those who are deprived of that blessing. Today, many hospitals and senior citizen's homes permit, and even welcome, animal visitors. Carefully chosen for their calm and friendly dispositions, these visitors interact with the patients and the elderly, sharing their animal essence, their serenity, their joy in just being. In some prisons, animals have played an important role in rehabilitation.

Of all the tales, my favorite is that of the little white dog who appeared at a large children's hospital in England. No one knew from where he came, but he gradually worked his way into the hearts of the staff. Every day he went around the wards visiting the patients. He always knew when a child was desperately sick and would spend hours curled up quietly on his or her bed, just being there. The children adored him.

One day a health inspector found the dog lying with a very ill child. Horrors! How unhygienic! So the little dog was banished from the wards. But his human friends still fed him outside. Meanwhile, the sick child had died. During the next few months the total number of deaths in the hospital rose steadily. Then one day, when a little girl was very ill indeed, one of the doctors, defying authority, let the little white dog into the ward. At once he jumped onto her bed and curled up next to her. The child smiled and she did not die after all. The dog was back where he belonged, and he was never turned out again.

If only all the dogs of the world could be as loved as Wisky Bisky is loved in my family. Sadly, of course, this is not so. For every dog that is loved and cared for there are thousands that are starved, beaten, mangy, and utterly miserable. It is not just the poor and ignorant who are guilty. Those who, without love or pity, slice, burn, and electrify dogs in our educational establishments and research labs are indeed blameworthy.

Throughout the world, in every country and every walk of life, there is a great deal of cruelty to animals. The fact that there is also a great deal of cruelty to human beings in no way excuses the cruelty to nonhuman beings. In some cases, cruelty to animals is deliberate, but often it is simply due to a lack of understanding. Thus, people can be cruel without realizing it because they do not know enough about the nature of nonhuman animals and their capacity for suffering. People can appear to condone cruelty when, in fact, they do not even know it is going on, though it may be taking place under their very noses.

Jane Goodall and Frodo

I have spent the past thirty-five years learning about our closest living relatives, the chimpanzees of Africa. When I first went to Tanzania, in 1960, no one suspected just how like us chimps really are. Chimpanzees kiss and embrace in greeting; pat subordinates gently to reassure them; hold hands with each other in moments of fear; swagger, punch and kick when they are angry. They can show empathy, compassion, and true altruism. They can reason and solve simple problems, as when they use tools for a whole variety of purposes in the wild. In captivity, they can learn and use several hundred of the signs of American Sign Language, used by people who cannot hear spoken language. Chimpanzees have a sense of humor and a concept of self.

There was a time when most people believed that a sharp line divided humans from the rest of the animal kingdom, but gradually over the years, that line has become increasingly blurred. Humans are unique, but we are not as different from some of the higher animals as once thought. Once we are prepared to admit that not only humans are capable of reason; not only humans know emotions like joy, fear, and despair; and above all, not only humans know mental as well as physical suffering, we will develop a new respect for the amazing nonhuman beings with whom we share this planet.

It is time we developed a new ethic in our attitude towards animals, especially in the industrialized societies of North America and Europe, where there is still a shocking abuse of pets. Some of it is deliberate: illegal dog fighting, puppy mills, and the horrendous manner in which some people train dogs, such as pit bulls, to be vicious fighters. There are countless dog owners who never should have taken on a dog at all, who do not have time for such a responsibility. Thousands and thousands of dogs are shut up all day long, with no chance of going out save a quick walk in the morning and another in the evening. There are dogs shut out in yards, sometimes chained, who never get a walk and seldom a kind word.

It is easy to start on an abuse list for cats, birds, rabbits, and other animals as well. All animals need space to run or climb or fly. They need attention, care, and time. These days it is possible to buy a whole array of exotic animals such as pythons, tropical birds, and monkeys. These animals should never be sold as pets, not unless the prospective owner has a complete understanding of their nature and needs, fully recognizes that they are likely to become increasingly unsuitable as they get older, and has the resources to provide proper care. No animals should ever be captured from the wild for pets; the live animal trade is responsible for unimaginable cruelty and suffering, and a truly horrific loss of life. Every time we buy an animal that started its life in the wild, we perpetrate that trade.

I have owned exotic animals. In Africa, where hunting of wildlife is commonplace, one sees monkeys or mongooses or other animals tied up in the market place or offered for sale at the side of the street. When I first went to Kenya, everyone quickly discovered I was crazy about animals, so all manner of living beings were brought to my apartment: two vervet monkeys, a bushbaby (or galago), two mongooses, a bat-eared fox, and others. Although they taught me a great deal and learned to trust their human guardian, almost every such adoption ended in tragedy. These animals belong in the wild, and for the most part, it is impossible to release them once they have become "tame."

There is also appalling abuse to which show horses are subjected. The same goes for animals who are trained for the entertainment industry. Circus people are beginning to speak out about this abuse. Kelly Tansy (who performs as a clown) is a young man who had the courage to describe some of the cruelty in public, especially involving chimpanzees. How fortunate it is that more people like Kelly are beginning to understand and to help.

People *are* helping in many ways. Some individuals make direct financial donations to a particular cause. Concerts are performed with the goal of raising money for animal rights organizations. Some artists are inspired to create works with a message that celebrate the beauty and wonder of nonhuman animals, and the need to care for them. More and more excellent documentary films are being produced. More books on the subject are being written and published.

Animal Magnetism combines the passion of two gifted photographers, Patti Denys and Mary Holmes (who also happen to be advocates for animals), with the willingness of a number of celebrities and prominent people to publicly declare their love of and commitment to animals. Patti and Mary use their photographic skills to advance public understanding not only of the value of animals in our lives, but of the worth of individual animals in their own right. I congratulate them, and their love shows through—their subjects, both human and nonhuman, are presented with dignity, compassion, and understanding.

Animal Magnetism presents an important message for everyone to consider: every individual matters, both human and nonhuman; every one of us has a role to play; and each of us can contribute, in a positive way, to the lives of those around us.

Jane Goodall

MICKEY *Rooney* & **Angel**

ANIMALS? WHERE WOULD OUR life be without the love of animals? When it comes to animals, all kinds of animals, any animals . . . they are the real human beings. We, people, are the animals. Did you know that if you spell dog backwards, it spells god?

I HAVE ALWAYS LOVED ANIMALS FOR AS LONG AS I can remember. Why, I do not exactly know. For one thing, animals, like children, have to live in a world that is not made for them. It is not even their size. Some of my own strongest memories could be straight from a day in any dog's life. Not being able to see the top of the table. Not being able to reach the cabinet. Not being able to open the kitchen door to go outside. Constant frustration. I know how they feel.

At the same time, I also think our animals are wiser than we are. I believe they know what is going on beneath the surface. Animals are channels of feeling, clear channels. I once was lucky enough to have a dog that was so intuitive I could count on her to assess people's moral characters, among other things. If she did not trust someone, I certainly was not about to. My life has become much more complicated and far lonelier since she died. It has been ten years now and I miss her every day.

"I THINK OUR ANIMALS ARE WISER THAN WE ARE."

CAROLINE *Thompson* & **Merrylegs**

CLEVELAND *Amory*
&Polar Star

I HAVE NEVER KNOWN A CAT I didn't love and admire, but I have to admit that Polar Star is something special. Living with his great elegance of person (yes, he is a person) as well as of mind and spirit, has been one of the most gratifying experiences of my life.

Jamie *Wyeth*
& Voler, Homer and Scud

Kleberg, 1984

Quite simply, I would rather be in the company of nonhumans. Given my druthers, I would choose to be alone. If accompanied, however, I would choose a pig, a sea gull, or a dog. As a consequence, the major body of my work is paintings of individuals either furred or feathered.

Flame has been really significant in my growth as a person. He came to me at a time in my life when I wasn't feeling great about myself and he really changed a lot for me. He makes me get out of bed in the morning whether I want to or not.

Flame has been a powerful influence in my life. I definitely think animals have spirits. My therapist told me to get a dog, and Flame really turned my life around.

One of the nicest compliments I ever got was when my boyfriend said, "You can't bring your dog everywhere. People are going to think you're eccentric." Well, I am! I am about my dog! He has special passes to get into buildings. If that doesn't work, I just say he's Lassie. It works in California. It doesn't work anywhere else, but it works out here.

Flame goes everywhere with me. He travels all over the world. He loves his little dog crate, because when he sees it out he knows he's going somewhere. Flame has been to Europe; he's been everywhere.

BEVERLY *Johnson* & Flame

BURGESS *Meredith* & Franchot

"I COUNT MYSELF FORTUNATE TO BE HIS PERSON."

FRANCHOT AND I have been close companions for some seventeen years. His mother, the lovely Picatso, long gone to glory, bore him on this same property, so he is understandably territorial. He has defended the homestead valiantly over the years and wears his many scars with dignity (his serrated ears, particularly).

His handsome good looks, charm, and the markings which give him the appearance of wearing evening clothes, caused me to name him after Franchot Tone, my close friend and a distinguished Hollywood leading man. Tone, Franchot, and I also had something in common: we all enjoyed a happily misspent youth raising carefree hell.

Franchot is a celebrity in his own right—he was chosen "Celebrity Cat of the Year" by Purina Cat Chow in 1985, and his formal portrait is on permanent exhibit at the local veterinarian's office.

We begin our day by sitting together at the breakfast table, where he helps me plan my day. In the evening, when I do not have any commitments, we settle down to watch a little television and catch up on world events.

When we retire he settles down at the foot of the bed. With typical sensitivity he keeps a discreet distance, so that we do not disturb each other.

Maturity has brought Franchot a serenity of spirit deeply soothing to those he honors with his friendship. I count myself fortunate to be his person.

N̄ot too long ago, I heard a politician on the California Senate floor say, "If God had meant animals to have rights, He would have given them!" Clearly, many people are uncomfortable with the idea of rights for animals. Luckily we are now witness to the world's emerging awareness of the simple rights of animals . . . to run if they have legs . . . to swim if they have fins . . . to fly if they have wings.

GRETCHEN *Wyler* & **Mikey**

WYLAND & Binky and Wy

Leap of Faith (Whaling Wall 57), 1994

THE ANIMALS, THE EARTH, AND ALL OF US ARE connected and equal in the eyes of God. These Jack Russells are really special; they were born the same month as I was. I am building a new place in Laguna for them because they really like the beach. They are beach dogs, which is a bit unusual for Jack Russells. These two really love the water and the ocean. It is a neat deal; they fulfill the circle of my life. I have a lot of good friends and a great family. Now I have great dogs. I have the best of everything. All I need now is a dolphin.

ROBERT *Pastorelli* & Friend

IF YOU ARE THINKING ABOUT ADOPTING A pet, you should go to the spcaLA (Society for the Prevention of Cruelty to Animals Los Angeles), where this kitty is from, or your local animal shelter. You are not only adopting, but also rescuing an animal. The breeding mills are substandard; if you buy from a pet store, you are supporting them.

"I CANNOT IMAGINE THAT THERE IS ANYONE WHO DOES NOT LOVE ANIMALS."

I AM YVONNE BRATHWAITE BURKE, SUPERVISOR OF THE 2ND DISTRICT OF LOS ANGELES County. After being out of politics for twelve years, I made the decision to come back to public service. I felt a need to combat many problems, particularly those of the inner city. I believe that most people who really care about other people also care about animals.

I cannot imagine that there is anyone who does not love animals. I have always had animals, and when I served in Congress, I traveled back and forth to Washington, D.C. every other week for six years, with a very small Yorkshire Terrier. I believe that animals are capable of real communication and give you a sense of caring. They are also very loyal.

One should go into public service to help solve the problems of the community, including issues of animal rights, and indeed, some of these problems are worldwide.

The Honorable
YVONNE *Burke*
&Bootsie

TONY *LaRussa* & Res

WHEN I WAS IN ARIZONA WITH THE OAKLAND A's, we trained at a community college for the first three weeks before going to the big ballpark to play games. The college was built on an Indian reservation in Scottsdale. One afternoon, the coaches and I were in the back room of the school's clubhouse when a boy walked in with a mutt, covered with ticks and fleas. The boy told us that the dog just walked in the front door. We took him to the vet and had him cleaned up. For a stray, he had the nicest personality. Because our two little poodles, that were formerly abused circus dogs, died in the last couple of years we did not have a dog. So we kept Res.

The athletes that I am around are marshmallows with dogs. When around dogs, no matter how hard the guy is, he just melts. Their machismo diffuses beautifully.

Whenever people ask me serious questions about the welfare of animals, I tell them about the Animal Rescue Foundation, the organization I founded in Contra Costa County, CA, that is dedicated to ensuring the humane treatment of animals and to bringing people and animals together to enrich each other's lives. It is hard for me to understand the moral fiber of society when people have the knowledge of what happens to an animal in order to make a fur coat, and they continue to buy those furs.

I am a straight arrow—I work hard, and I believe in the basic values of life. I think there are a lot of people in this country who are similar to me, who love and care for their animals. My goal is to provide people with information about animal rights and to give them the knowledge they need to make intelligent decisions about how to treat animals properly.

BEATRICE *Wood* & Rajah

"I TELL EACH OF MY DOGS THAT HE IS THE NICEST DOG IN THE WORLD."

My love of animals started when I was a little girl and read a story about a soldier in battle who loved his horse. The soldier had nowhere to sleep but against the belly of his horse. This story touched me so much that ever since, I have wanted a horse in my bed. So I have compromised with dogs and cats. They are like little children who come to me for protection. I tell each of my dogs that he is the nicest dog in the world. I believe that is not a lie, for in that moment, he is.

Untitled, 1996

JOEL *Grey* & Betty

I CANNOT IMAGINE LIFE WITHOUT AN ANIMAL TO LOVE. YOU LEARN SO MUCH ABOUT YOURSELF and about nature. Living with Betty is like living with a wild cat because as tame as she is, adapted and adaptive,

you know that inside of this house cat is a very primitive being. She displays that instinct, whether it is by a jump, a leap, or a turn.

When she sees a bird, and I hear those guttural sounds that suddenly come out of this "houseified" cat, I know that she is some creature from nature that I am privileged to live alongside. In our technological world, a creature of this natural complexity is such a gift.

RUE *McClanahan*
& Polly, Winston, Angie, Belle, Ginger and Jackson

IF IT WEREN'T FOR MY MARVELOUS, FUNNY, LOVING DOGS AND CATS, I WOULD PROBABLY HAVE flipped my wig years ago. God love 'em one and all!!!

INGRID *Newkirk*
Bill E. Goat, Harry and Sammy

WE ARE ALL ANIMALS. WHO CARES WHAT SHAPE or size we come in? Chicken or child, we all need love and comfort, we all hope to avoid fear and pain, and we all appreciate kindness. As the species at the top of the heap, only we can protect those that are not so lucky; many of whom are not just less comfortable than we are, but deprived of every pleasure, sometimes even their lives, because of our bad habits and our thoughtlessness.

Animals are whole and wonderful. They are not ours to eat, wear, experiment on, or use for entertainment.

"ANIMALS ARE WHOLE AND WONDERFUL."

Loretta *Swit* & Ten Man

"IF WE ALLOW IT, ANIMALS BRING OUT THE BEST IN US."

Wildlife protection, the environment, and animal welfare are top priorities on my schedule. Among my friends I count orangutans, boa constrictors, Bengal tigers, sea lions, a snow leopard, an eagle, a wolf, and a cerval. I have met them all nose-to-nose and one-on-one. I love and respect them all and will always work to protect their welfare.

Ten Man and I spend most mornings together; he is a loving, devoted animal friend who is markedly depressed when I go on location. Our camaraderie is best displayed when we jump over fences together in sync, in rhythm—bonding like one animal. We both enjoy riding and physical eloquence. Someone very wise once said, "The best thing for the insides of a (wo)man is the outsides of a horse." If we allow it, animals bring out the best in us.

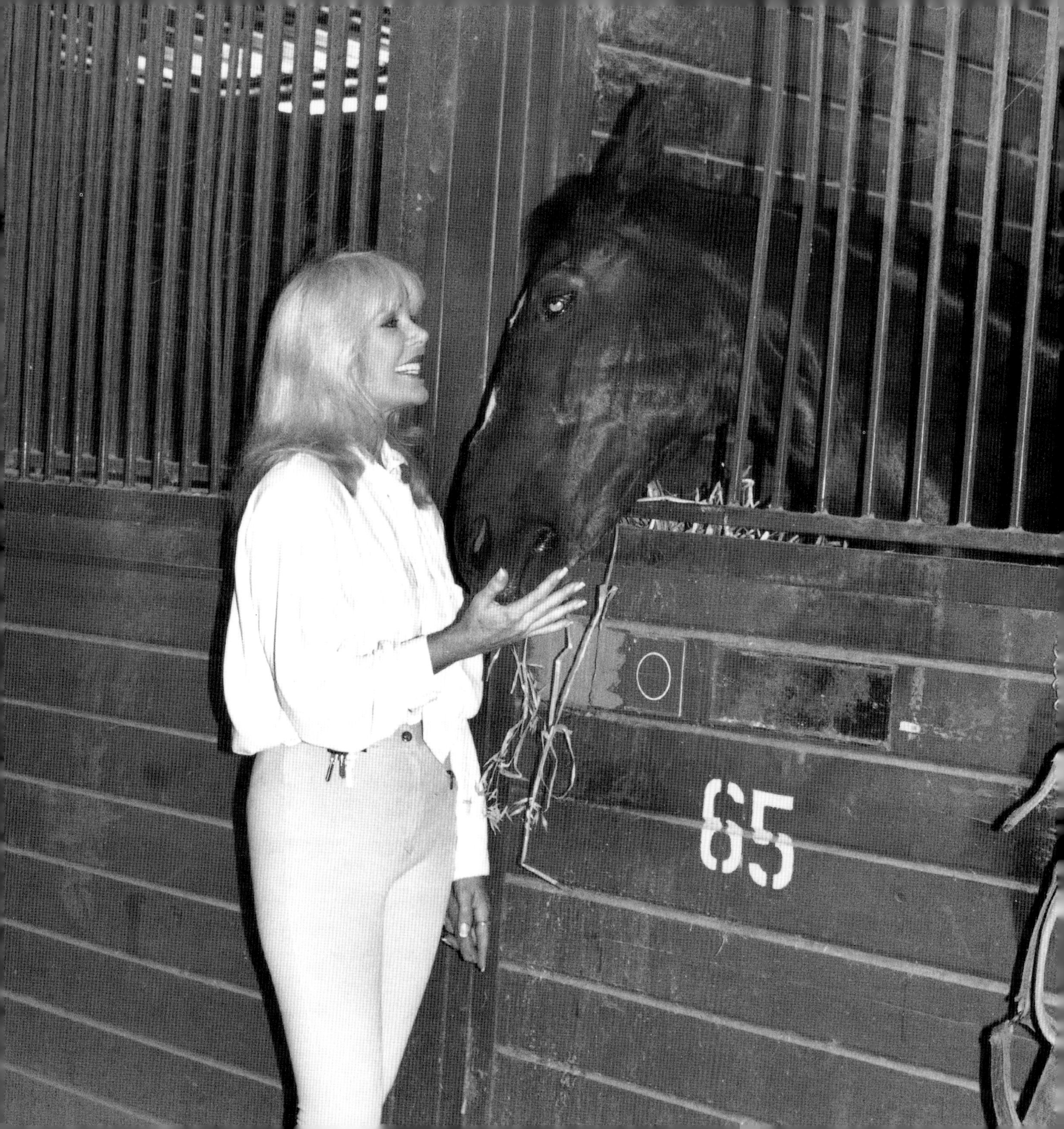
65

I THINK OF OUR RELATIONSHIP WITH animals as being very fundamental to our place on the planet and to understanding how we all fit together. I have always had animals. I grew up with a lot of cats and a few dogs. I am particularly drawn to cats; I adore them. I once had an animal named Ruffles who died of a heart ailment. After he died, I immediately ran out to get these two guys. I have brought home strays and have been given some. Sometimes I find them in pounds or in shops, as was the case with these two.

I think that if people had a close relationship with an animal, they could not possibly hunt. When some friends told me that they were going hunting for birds in Europe, I laughingly said, "Those are my birds, too, you know, they're not just yours. I do not know what gives you the idea you can hunt such beautiful creatures in Europe and not offend my life."

I have always been fascinated by the relationship between animals and human beings because I think we have so much to learn about our nonverbal communication. I have a friend who goes on travel

adventures, one of which took him to Baja to look at whales. He says the most exciting thing in his life was seeing a whale eye-to-eye. I had a similar connection when I went to Montauk, the furthest point on Long Island, and went whale watching. I love animals, and I like to see them cared for and cared about. When I spend time with my cats, they are so loving and communicative. They like to make you happy to be with them and they do it wonderfully. If we all did this as well as cats do, what a peaceful life we would have.

JUDY *Collins*
Sunshine and Midnight

WHETHER SHE IS WEARING her faux pearls at a snappy dinner party or hiking the snow-covered trails of our mountain retreat, Phoebe teaches me understanding for creatures great and small, compassion for those who go it alone, trust in instinct, the importance of sharing both time and substance, and the value of an afternoon nap.

THOMAS *Schumacher* & **Phoebe**

BOB *Hope* & Snowell and Junior

H OW DO YOU LIKE THESE GUYS? MY DAUGHTER LINDA GAVE THEM TO ME AS A PRESENT A couple of years ago, and they have been beautiful ever since. I take them down to Palm Springs. I can even get them to sing.

AUDREY *Flack* & Isis

I NAME MY ANIMALS AFTER ARTISTS. ELAINE de Kooning had a dog named Jackson; we know who he was named after. I once had a poodle named Angelica Kaufman after the 18th-century French artist. My yellow-naped Amazon parrot was named Albert Einstein Bierstadt for all of the great Alberts.

But Isis was the name already given to my bird while in the pet shop, which is kind of amazing since I did a painting called *Isis*. She is a black-capped conure with a wide black-and-white design that circles around her neck like an Egyptian necklace. A line of brilliant geranium red glows from under her wings and the rest of her body is iridescent green.

She is very demanding and wants to have her head rubbed all the time. She is also quite intelligent. Isis sits on my shoulder while I work or crawls into my shirt where she remains with her beak sticking out as if she were in a papoose.

What else can I tell you? She is filled with love. She eats supper with my family and has orange juice with me every morning, and she just hangs out.

Artists tend to lead solitary lives working in their studios. Isis has become my companion. This tiny being really loves me and I love her. We are bonded.

Reynolda House, Museum of American Art, Winston-Salem, N.C.

Bounty, 1978

TIONNE *Watkins* & Butchie

ONE THING ABOUT MY DOGS IS THAT they make me feel better. I know they love me unconditionally. If I am upset, Butchie and Apache (not pictured) are always there like they do not care how awful I am at times. When I am mad at everyone, Butchie and Apache still be cool with me.

SONNY *Barger*
& Sadie and
Reinfield

I LIKE ALL ANIMALS. WE have squirrels, raccoons, cats, and dogs. I guess it is cliché to say this, but, if my dogs don't like 'em, I do not trust 'em.

WE HAVE HAD THE PLEASURE OF SHARING OUR home with four cats. It breaks my heart to think of the seventeen million dogs and cats that are killed yearly in our shelters for the crime of not having a home. Spaying and neutering is so simple, and it's a matter of life or death. Eighty percent of the animals entering the shelters are euthanized, a staggering number in a civilized country! It is abominable that we continue breeding cats and dogs while we are killing them due to overpopulation. I confess that I lose respect for people that buy animals from breeders because it keeps that rotten industry alive. I have been involved with trapping, spaying, and releasing numerous feral (or wild) cats. If you have feral cats living in your area, please feed them, and just as important, borrow a humane trap from your local shelter so you can take the cats to be spayed or neutered. These cats are so often ignored and live their lives close to starvation because our society views them as pests. Remember, feral cats are the children of strays, left behind by unkind or insensitive owners to breed and survive in trashcans. Perhaps someday we will learn.

—*Kevin Nealon*

THE ISSUE THAT IS MOST IMPORTANT TO ME is our "food animals," because these animals are killed by the billions annually in the most cruel and barbaric ways. Eating dead animals is the primary cause of heart disease, cancer, and strokes; in fact, if all people were to switch to a vegetarian diet (without fish and poultry) seventy-five percent of deaths from heart attacks would be eliminated. If there was a drug that could do the same, it would be all over the news!

I think we need to bring our children on field trips to slaughterhouses before they are desensitized, and give them a choice about what they want to eat. There would be a lot more happy animals living in this world.

—*Linda Nealon*

KEVIN *Nealon*
LINDA & *Nealon*
Ellie, Molly and
Pierre Perot

VICKI *Lawrence*
& Candy and Max

"ANIMALS ARE GREAT EQUALIZERS."

MY DOGS GIVE ME UNCONDITIONAL LOVE. THEY ARE REALLY GOOD AT BRINGING ME BACK DOWN

to earth, too. I think they are great at helping me realize what my priorities are and what is real, particularly when

they have left me a "present" in the middle of the living room floor. Animals are great equalizers.

Lᴏʟᴀ ɪꜱ ɴᴇꜰᴇʀᴛɪᴛɪ ʀᴇɪɴᴄᴀʀɴᴀᴛᴇᴅ.

Lola and I, in our later years, have become closer. She is fourteen, and God knows what I am. Lola has been photographed by some very well-known photographers. She is probably the most photographed cat in Taos.

The younger my dogs, Cindy and Peter, are, the younger I feel. Lola is older than they are. But they are not as civilized.

Honky, 1995

Lola, 1995

R.C. Gorman & Lola

MICHELLE *Phillips* & Mika

WHAT CAN I SAY? MIKA IS MY DEAREST AND CLOSEST

friend. And she is mine. She is the doggiest dog in all of

doggerdom, and she knows it. She is the doggus. Mika and I

communicate on a very spiritual level—food.

ELLIOTT *Gould*
&Grace

I ONCE HAD A DOG NAMED HUMPHREY. SINCE HUMPHREY DID NOT LIKE BEING ON A LEASH, it was quite provocative and unconventional to have this divine crossbreed of a canine in New York City. On a sunny afternoon in April a few years ago, we walked down Fifth Avenue at 57th Street with traffic going one way down the Avenue, and two ways across the street. It is dangerous to be alive in a world of people and cars.

On another day, we were having a lovely and peaceful stroll through the West Village near Morton Street and came upon a handsome German Shepherd on a leash. The dog was lying next to his master who was sitting on a chair next to a building. This time I was ahead of Humphrey who was walking with my friend Jenny. When the German Shepherd became aware of Humphrey he understandably became agitated and upset. His owner pulled the leash in until there was no more slack. By now, the Shepherd was viciously and violently snarling and barking at Humphrey. Humphrey calmly and seemingly bemused, walked up to the unhappy purebred German Shepherd's face, looked at him and seemed to muse, "Gee whiz, I wish you weren't so upset by me. Why not just relax? Enjoy yourself. Cool out. Don't take life so seriously."

SUE *Coe* & Bandit

MY FRIENDS, THE RATS, LIVE ON A HIGHER plane than I do. I sit and watch TV; they sit and watch me. There is a Ratorama built in my apartment—swings, slides, ladders, and a teapot in which they live. As they are of a laboratory rat species, they appreciate all the freedom. If the rats could train me to come and play at the ring of a bell, the bell would be ringing all the time. They like sitting on my shoulder and seeing new sights; I have to watch out for flying rats, as they take off from one of the swings to land on a shoulder. Occasionally the target is missed, and there is a degree of rat embarrassment, which is always bluffed over.

In the morning when I open my eyes, there are six rat eyes staring and willing me to get up and play. They all get in bed, and run up and down like maniacs under the covers, until exhausted; they collapse in a rat heap. When they sleep, they twitch their whiskers like brushes and they clench their tiny hands.

Rats are very clean—they constantly wash their faces and ears. Rats smell nice, better than any bottled perfume. The strange thing is, although rats are mute (apart from an occasional squeak when they get hurt), they can understand human language. In fact, the rats seem to understand my thoughts before they are vocalized.

I have seen rats in a laboratory, their entire lives spent in a tiny cage with no nesting material, no contact with each other. They are bred to develop cancer, be cut open, and sewn back up. I have seen photographs of heads of rats sewn onto other rat bodies. A human has to have quite an imagination to be evil. The scientists who breed these rats to get cancer are worse than evil.

They Made Themselves Extinct, 1997

GREG *Louganis*

& Brutus, Ryan Luke, Leilani and Donna

WHY DO PEOPLE LIE AND DECEIVE?
Dogs don't.
If they don't like you, they
bark, growl, or bite.
If they like you,
they lick, jump, and wag
their tails,
just wanting to be with you.
There's a lot to be learned
from dogs.

EARL *Holliman* & Randy and Blondie

MY PARENTS, HENRY AND VELMA HOLLIMAN, TAUGHT ME TO LOVE AND RESPECT ANIMALS.

When I was eleven, I had a lot of school chums. But, when they were not around, I also had my dogs, Lady and Tatters; my cats, Honey and Cheeta; my goat, Napoleon; and my pig, Alexander. I raised them all and I think they all loved me. Although I was an only child, I never felt lonely.

Today, I suppose I am the old man that the eleven year-old me never thought I would be. I still have lots of friends. But, when they are not around, I also have my dogs, Randy, Blondie, and Farley, and my cats, Tom, Mister, Jennie, Monroe, Alice, and Maybelle. I love them all. And I think they all love me. I still never get lonely. . . .

I think maybe my parents knew what they were doing.

"MY PARENTS TAUGHT ME TO LOVE AND RESPECT ANIMALS."

74

MY ANIMALS are my family. It is Rich, me, Ying, Yang, Reno, and Jonathan.

BARBARA *Bach Starkey*

Ying, Yang & and Reno

JUDY *Chicago*
& Sebastian and Romeo

WHEN I WAS WORKING ON THE HOLOCAUST PROJECT, I began to question our whole treatment of animals. When I visited Auschwitz, I saw that it was a giant processing plant, but instead of processing pigs they processed people. They actually applied the same principles that are used in terms of the processing of animals to the processing of people. It was at that point I became horrified and shocked, and asked, "How could this happen?"

Thinking about that led me to look at our treatment of animals on the planet. It also caused me to personally change my way of living and eating. However, I recognized that it was very difficult to create a personal solution to a larger moral and ethical problem—that human beings live on this planet at the expense of all the other species. And, because we have assumed that we are at the top of a pyramid that exists for our sole use, we haven't questioned very thoroughly our relationship to other species.

During the Holocaust, these larger issues of dominance were applied to Jews; they were cast into the roles of pigs or cats or creatures that were used up. In fact, there is a German word *vermaagt* that means "used-up," and this was the concept for how Jews were to be treated. They were to be used up for whatever the Nazis could get out of them—their gold teeth, their labor, and their bodies for fertilizer. This is what we do to animals all the time, we use them up. I did not expect this revelation to happen as a result of looking at the Holocaust, but it caused me to question: what does it mean to commemorate the Holocaust if in fact we do not actually learn the lessons it teaches us?

Would You Wear Your Dog?, 1992

LAUREN *Shuler-Donner* & RICHARD *Donner*

Buster, Ralph, Samantha and Gracie

"PEOPLE COULD LEARN A LOT FROM DOGS."

PEOPLE WHO RESPECT ANIMALS SEEM TO HAVE GREAT SELF-RESPECT. I TRULY BELIEVE THAT many people have no real respect for living things other than human life. When they learn to respect all life, including animals, they will then have a different attitude toward one another. Animals will then become even more of a mirror of how men and women feel about each other.

—Richard Donner

THESE ANIMALS ARE OUR FOUR BEST FRIENDS. EVERY TIME THEY GREET US, THEY ARE wonderfully excited to see us. They wag their tails, so we know they are happy. They come over and nudge us when they need affection. They are loyal team players and they like to have fun. People could learn a lot from dogs.

—Lauren Shuler-Donner

ALEX *Pacheco*
& Rocky and Lily

Is it so difficult to extend to all living beings the compassion we wish for ourselves? Until we create a cruelty-free world for all animals, we must continue to work for justice for animals, continue to fight for their rights, and continue to care. I find personal strength in Victor Hugo's observation that, "Nothing else in the world. . . Not all the armies is so powerful as an idea whose time has come." The time for animal rights is now!

ACTUALLY, THIS IS WHAT BUDDY ASKED ME to say. This is a wonderful quote about cats from the French writer and critic, Théophile Gautier.

"Who can believe that there is no soul behind those luminous eyes?"

MIMI *Rogers* & **Buddy**

DANNY *Elfman* & **Gus**

In these first six months of his life, Gus seems to be fitting in quite well with my lifestyle. He is moody, he sulks a lot, and he sleeps as late as I do. Like all great dogs, he directly counters my everlasting pessimism with his divine canine optimism.

WILLIAM *Wegman* & **Fay** and **Batty**

WHEN MAN RAY DIED, I DIDN'T WANT TO GET another dog. He had given me twelve wonderful years as both animal companion and art partner, and the thought of trying to replace him was unthinkable. Five years later in Memphis, Tennessee, I met a femme fatale. I named her Fay Ray.

I had no intention of photographing Fay as I had Man Ray, and I abstained from doing so for a year. Then, for no apparent reason, I took her to the Polaroid photo studio with me and she really took to the camera. I realized that I had been denying both of us something she really liked doing, so I dove into it wholeheartedly.

When Fay had her seven puppies, I started working a lot with two of them: Chundo, who I gave to my sister, and Batty here. I noticed how different their personalities were and started to construct works devoted to the individual dog. I noticed how different Fay was from Ray, but more clearly how different Battina was from Fay and the others. When I did the book *Cinderella*, I cast them as characters based on their personalities as I had come to know them.

When they are on, they are on. I never spontaneously say, "I think I'll take your picture now. You look nice over there." Instead, we will go into the studio, set up the lights, and do something. They really act as professionals. It is not that far-fetched to call them that because this is their job: they do it, and I think they like it, because they would not do it if they didn't like it. I think dogs need something to do. The worst thing you can do is leave them at home while you go off to work and deny then their independence, which unfortunately, most people have to do. I get to take the dogs to work with me.

I would not deny that some of the pictures are really funny. But, when I am working with them, it is more like a dance, a freestyle give and take. I do not think, "Oh, this will be funny," or, "Isn't this stupid, I'll have them do this." I don't see our relationship as that strange, either. I have been photographing my dogs for twenty-three years, how could it be strange?

Untitled, 1994

"MY OWN CONVICTION IS that the study of human physiology by way of experiments on animals is the most grotesque and fantastic error ever committed in the whole range of human intellectual activity."

—*G.F. Walker*

My opinion exactly.

GRACE *Slick* & Bucky

SID *Caesar*
& Plato and Minnie

PLATO AND MINNIE ARE the best friends I have. I love them and they love me. When I come home at night, aaaah, there is nothing better. A little love, a little food, and you have got friends for life.

If you want animal friends, please get them from the pound—they appreciate it.

SARA *Gilbert* & Ralph

VEGETARIANISM IS THE

least I can do in the

crusade to save the animals.

ALEXANDRA *Day*
& Sprocket and Arambarri

CHILDREN SEEM TO FEEL A NATURAL KINSHIP with animals, and I was no exception. I talked to my dogs and horses, played with them, loved them, and was loved by them. We understood each other remarkably well. To me, animals seemed like dependent and trustful younger brothers and sisters. They still do. The idea of killing or eating animals, or experimenting on them, repels me because of my view.

It has always puzzled me that most people seem to share my feelings in regard to their particular pet animals, but fail to extend this consciousness to animals in general. People would be outraged at the thought of eating their own dog or experimenting on their own cat, but they never think to object to the slaughtering of the lamb they have never met or the torturing of the dog next door in a laboratory.

Just as we recognize a private duty to our own children, and a social duty toward all children, our love for the pet animals we know should lead us to a concern for the welfare of all animals.

Carl's Birthday, 1995

JAMES *Cromwell* & Colin

WORKING ON *BABE* INFLUENCED ME BECAUSE WHEN talking to people about the film, I felt as though I had to apologize to them for consuming animals. I had been a vegetarian for many years, but when I began to race bicycles I found that I could not get enough protein, and I was allergic to the carbohydrates I ate. I did not want someone to say, "Mr. Cromwell, are you a vegetarian?" I would have had to answer, "No, actually my lifestyle mitigates my being a vegetarian." When I worked on *Babe*, I wanted one of the main messages of the film to be the upholding and preserving of the dignity of life, including all animal life. So, I went all the way and became a vegan.

People might think that making the choice to become vegan, which is a life choice, is easy. However, everything has to change: your attitude toward yourself, your attitude toward those who live with you, your work, the community as a whole, and what your responsibilities are.

I am primarily concerned about the factory farm system. I believe if people actually knew what went into the processing of meat, nobody would eat it. When you go to a processing farm and see horses being dragged by their hooves to be stunned and cut up for consumption, you have to wonder if people are crazy. Some of these horses were pets. If you can love a horse as a pet, you would never think of eating him.

Becoming a vegetarian or vegan is a new beginning for many people. It is a way to take responsibility for the world and influence the way we want it to be. When people start to change their lives, they soon realize that they are not only making a difference in their own lives, but they are making a difference in the world around them. I believe my choice was an idea whose time had come. A vegan or vegetarian lifestyle could change the world, and if we all applied it, we would change the world.

It is really nice when you have the opportunity to do a movie like *Babe*. You can let the best part of you, the most vulnerable, honest, caring, loving, supportive, concerned part of you, out. You have the potential to become a role model, and that is a very powerful thing.

One of the few negative comments I heard about the film, is actually positive. A woman wrote to a magazine to complain about *Babe* after taking her family to see it. She enjoyed the movie, but when her family returned home, her daughter informed her that she would no longer eat meat. She tried to convince her daughter otherwise and became upset that this little comedic film caused her family to confront an issue that she did not want to. My motto is and always will be:

PLEASE DO NOT EAT ANIMALS.

THE NICE PART OF WORKING WITH A dog like Lassie is that it is wholesome, meaningful, and rewarding. You develop a great relationship with a dog when you make movies with her, but you are also doing something that is emotional, involves people, and sends a positive message. That is why we like to work with and watch Lassie—she is such a positive role model.

ROBERT *Weatherwax* & Lassie

ROBERT *Rauschenberg*

& Toma, Sasha, Chung, Opal and Misha

Prego (Urban Bourbon Series), 1991

BESIDES DOGS, I HAVE A NYC LIVE-IN TURTLE, ROCKEY, that has been in residence since 1965. I once had twenty-six cats unintentionally. My most exotic love was Sweetie, a kinkajou that lived and traveled with me. The exchange for enduring all the complexities, joy + pain, is love unmeasurably given + received more + more + more. My age can be counted in litters.

TONY *Curtis*
JILL *Vandenberg*
& Josephine, Daphne and Bodie

OUR DOGS ARE OUR FRIENDS.

We share our living experience together:

the good, the bad, and the ugly. It is more

like, the good, the bad, and the scooper!

JANE *Goodall, Ph.D.* & Frodo

FOR THIRTY-FIVE YEARS, I HAVE HAD THE privilege of studying and often living with a community of wild chimpanzees, our closest living relatives. The most important thing I have learned from them is humility. Humans are a unique species, but we are not as different as we think. There is no unbridgeable chasm separating us from the rest of the animal kingdom. Chimpanzees teach us that not only humans have distinct personalities; not only humans are capable of rational thought; and not only humans show emotions similar or identical to those we describe as joy, sadness, fear, and despair. Not only humans suffer mentally and physically.

This knowledge leads us to a new understanding of and respect for all of the other amazing nonhuman animals with which we share the planet. It also raises ethical considerations about the way we use and abuse animals each day.

How can we bother with "mere" animals when there is so much human suffering? Cruelty is one of the worst of our sins. Children who are cruel to animals typically become cruel adults—cruelty affects the perpetrator as well as the victim.

To attain our true human potential, to become more compassionate and loving, we must care about all sentient, sapient beings. If the rain forests and the wild places disappear, if the desert creeps relentlessly forward, if the level of pollution rises and the hole in the ozone layer increases, and if the number of people in the world continues to multiply, it is not only nonhuman animals, but people who will suffer. They are suffering already.

"ONLY IF WE UNDERSTAND CAN WE CARE ONLY IF WE CARE WE SHALL HELP ONLY IF WE HELP SHALL WE BE SAVED."

W<small>ELL, DOGS ARE LOVELY, SOFT,</small> cuddly creatures. I do think they are gorgeous creatures. Apart from not eating red meat, I don't know quite what to say. I find that. . . I love them. Yes, I love them very much.

D<small>UDLEY</small> *Moore* & Chelsea and Minka

Matuschka & Liberty

The most life-altering experience I had after being diagnosed with cancer was when I eliminated all animal products from my diet, including dairy. I did this as a life-saving measure, and as my health and appearance improved and changed, so did my attitude toward nature (rocks included) and all living species.

> Treat everything equal
> as you are of no more in value
> than that ant crossing the road
> who actually may need
> more attention
> as he is ignorant of death
> by a moving tire

In some ways, cancer led me to use my art in a more responsible way. My involvement in environmental art and animal rights also inspired me to create images that questioned man's polluting and tampering with nature.

> "Now, the question is about mosquitos
> that buzz by and bite me
> should I learn not to swat them
> and let them take the specimen
> (my blood) for free?"

Alabama Dog, 1989

Max *Perlich* & Redd

REDD IS MY FIRST SON.
I tried for many, many
years to bear a child, and
Redd just popped out. We
are doing pretty well.
Sometimes he gets into
trouble, but he is my one
and only love other than
my mother and my
'53 Chevy.

MARY *Frann* & Panache

A WHILE AGO, I HAD BEEN TRYING TO FIND A DOG AND PARTICULARLY wanted to rescue a dog. I thought that if I had a little dog, I could bring it to the set every day with me. If I could rescue a dog, that would be all the more meaningful. When I met Panache, the woman who owned him said, "Well, you know, he gets up at 5:30 every morning. He will wake you up." I thought, I am not a morning person at all. I am completely a night person. Even so, I took the dog immediately.

From that night on, when I slept in, the dog slept in. They say that dogs take on the characteristics of their humans—this was true of Panache right from the beginning. We bonded immediately. He eats late; I eat late. It is a riot.

There is something that is healing to the spirit about living with an animal because of the unconditional love they provide. Animals depend on you to take care of them and you find yourself, as I have discovered, dependent on that unconditional love.

Many times I have entered the house feeling as if little pieces of me had fallen off on the freeway, only to come home and have Panache greet me with such excitement. I know it may sound trite, but caring for an animal really is healing because animals fill in a lot of gaps. They want to bond with you.

When we talk about unconditional love we must also talk about responsibility. If you choose to have an animal live with you, you do have the responsibility to take care of it. This means spaying or neutering it. The animal is in your care, and it is your responsibility to make sure that it is healthy, well-fed, and treated like the special creature it is.

MONTY *Roberts* & Dually

IF I HAD BUT ONE CHOICE of a theme, it would be that no one has the right to say, "you must" to another person or to an animal. You can say, "I wish you would, I would like you to, and the following consequences might occur if you do not," but no pain, no restraint, no hitting, and no kicking should occur when you train an animal.

I believe that a good trainer can get a horse to do what he wants him to do. A great trainer can cause the horse to want to do it.

Shera Danese *Falk*
& Zelda, Scarlet, Giovinna and Peteie

My second rescued dog, Scarlet, appeared to me in a dream. I was taking an acting class at the time, and one of our exercises for class was to force a dream, or make a dream come to us, and she was in the dream. What is really funny is that it was supposed to be a dream about love, a romantic dream, with a man in it. Instead, I dreamt about a dog.

Following our acting class instructor's instructions, I chanted something before I went to sleep to bring on the dream. While sleeping, I dreamt of a big dog standing over me in bed. The dog was very wolf-like.

Two weeks later, I found Scarlet. When I woke up the morning after finding her, there she was, standing over me exactly like the dog in my dream. Even though she hardly resembles a wolf, I knew the minute I saw her standing there that she was the dog from my dream.

PETER *Vidmar*
&Thunder

"IT IS IMPORTANT TO SPAY AND NEUTER YOUR ANIMALS."

OUR ANIMAL COMPANIONS ARE REALLY A PART OF our family. I think it is wonderful for children to be around animals; they learn to appreciate them as members of the family. I also strongly believe that we have certain responsibilities toward our animal companions. It is very important that people who are considering purchasing dogs or cats think very strongly about the time they are going to spend with the animal, the size of their home, the size of their yard, and the type of affection and care they can give the animal.

Also, it is important to spay or neuter your animals. This ensures that you will not cause lives to come into the world and add to animal overpopulation.

Rachel *Rosenthal*

& Hytoo and Barney Bear

We abuse, enslave, and exploit animals in every possible way because of our christian and cartesian philosophical heritage, which predicates that animals have neither feelings nor souls.

Science now shows us in ample ways that animals think, feel, and express themselves in specific ways that parallel language. We must shed our belief that we are the top of the biological pyramid and therefore are permitted to do with others as we please, and accept our place as one link in the chain of life on Earth. We must treat animals with respect and justice, and learn from them the countless things they have to teach us. In other words, we must at last become willing to shed our hubris vis-à-vis other species.

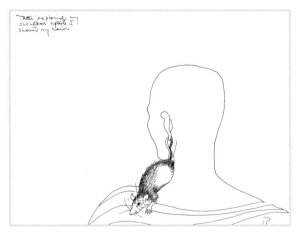

Tatti Exploring My Shoulder
After I Shaved My Head, 1996

ENGELBERT *Humperdinck*
LOUISE *Dorsey*
Chico, Harry and Tess

"WE ARE A WELL-ROUNDED, PREJUDICE-FREE, ANIMAL-LOVING FAMILY."

OUR LIVES HAVE BEEN TRULY BLESSED BY THE ANIMALS that have shared their years with us. Every one of them has been such a character, digging deeply into our memories, as well as the garden! To date, we have had a Dalmatian, two Pugs, a 300-pound St. Bernard, five German Shepherds, two Jack Russells, two Belgian Shepherds with German accents, a Cockapoo from Encino, a Jack Russell's child that was fathered while awandering, a Lab of questionable origin, a Golden Retriever that also fancies himself as a Brittany Spaniel, four cats, a rabbit, and a handful of ferrets. We are a well-rounded, prejudice-free, animal-loving family.

Our first family dog, the Dalmatian, used to get arrested all the time for stealing the neighbors' bread after the milkman delivered it to their doorstep. We actually have pictures of him being bailed out from the local jail, paws on the sign-out desk, giving the bobby a smile that meant, "See you next week, mate!" I could go on and on about our eclectic, mostly beautiful, but sometimes motley crew, but that is a book in itself.

Harry, Tess, and Chico are currently residing at the Pink Palace in Los Angeles. Harry was separated from his brother William, due to sibling rivalry. William was forced to maintain his residency at our home in England with the British bunch.

If one were to look in the mirror, one would see the most dangerous animal on earth.

Lee *Starkey*

& Daisy and Big Boss

Marc Davis
Miss Chris and Virgil

ONE OF THE REASONS I ORIGINALLY WENT TO WALT DISNEY STUDIO AND APPLIED FOR WORK was that I was an expert at drawing animals. I had studied their anatomies and I spent a lot of time in zoos— I traveled everywhere under the sun. When I came down to the studio I proved that I could draw animals much better than most of the other illustrators, but I ended up doing the human characters because they had to be believable also.

It was not until I worked on *Bambi* that I had a chance to draw structured animals. I think the book, *Disney Animation: The Illusion of Life* by Frank Thomas and Ollie Johnston, speaks about the vitality that I find in drawing animals. The book is an important part of what happened to animation at that time. When the animals were drawn for *Snow White and the Seven Dwarfs*, they did not have the structured vitality that was really necessary for a film like *Bambi*.

MARTINA *Navratilova*

& Puma, K.D. and Yoni

GANDHI ONCE SAID, "THE GREATNESS OF A nation and its moral progress can be judged by the way its animals are treated." It still amazes me that people can differentiate between a cow and a dog.

Of course, you have to draw the line somewhere and some people draw it where they do not eat any animals; some just do not eat cows, some do not eat pigs, whatever. I think everybody can push that line a little further than where it is today. I am trying to eliminate dairy products from my diet. Those cows that ran around had a life. I think we owe it to the animals to give them a life, even if we do slaughter them, they should at least have a good quality of life while they are awaiting their deaths.

A lot of people say, "Oh well, I know they are treated terribly, but I don't want to know about it. I don't want to go to a slaughterhouse." They will not go because they know that if they went, they would never eat meat.

They do not want to know about what happens in slaughterhouses, so they can still eat meat and not feel guilty. Most animal farms are completely cruel and have no regard for the animals on them, only how much meat or eggs or milk they can get in as short a period of time to make as big a profit as possible.

Omitting meat from my diet has been a very gradual process. First it was veal, twelve to thirteen years ago, and then it was complete vegetarianism. What pushed me is that I did not want to be a hypocrite. I decided if I am not willing to shoot it myself, I should not be willing to eat it.

I wish people would become more aware and draw the line a little further. I know people who have a pot-bellied pig for a pet and they still eat pork. How can you do that? It is like eating your dog. How do you differentiate? So, I just wish people would draw that line a little further.

DAVID *Ellefson*
&Buffy and Sugie

"I ENJOY BEING A VEGETARIAN; IT IS ANOTHER EXPRESSION OF MY LOVE FOR ANIMALS."

I HAVE BEEN AN ANIMAL LOVER SINCE I WAS A CHILD. I BECAME INTERESTED IN PERSIAN CATS nearly five years ago. I have had four different Persians since then, and I have given a couple to my mother. Now I have these two.

Ironically enough, heavy metal led me to vegetarianism. After getting clean and sober from all drugs, alcohol, and cigarettes several years ago, vegetarianism became another extension of the spiritual, mental, and physical side of improving myself.

It all came to a head for me in the early part of 1993 when Megadeth received the Doris Day Music Award from the Ark Trust for our album, *Countdown to Extinction*. The night of the award ceremony really pushed me over the edge. I had been gradually eliminating meat from my diet, and at that point it became obvious to me that I should do it not only for health reasons, but also because I love animals. I realized I no longer wanted to eat them. I truly believe in karmic reaction, that if I do good unto animals, they will in turn do good unto me. I enjoy being a vegetarian; it is another expression of my love for animals.

PAUL *Watson* & Piglet

I DON'T BELIEVE IN HAVING PETS AT ALL, SO I have never really had a pet. Occasionally we get animals that we find on the ship or at sea. This pigeon was found up in the main mast. Its mother had laid some eggs that had just recently hatched when we left Halifax. We didn't discover the baby pigeon until a few days later when a plane that was doing surveillance on us flew low overhead, and we went up to the mast to photograph it. On the way up, one of the crew heard the pigeons squealing. This one managed to survive. We're going to rehabilitate it and put it back in the wild.

I started *Sea Shepherd* in 1977, and since then, we have had numerous ships and campaigns. The campaigns have been worldwide; we are probably responsible for protecting tens of thousands of whales, hundreds of thousands of dolphins, and millions of seals.

The *Sea Shepherd Conservation Society* is an international marine wildlife conservation enforcement organization, so we are the only international marine enforcement agency in existence. There are a lot of laws, regulations, and treaties on the books, but they do not mean anything unless people are enforcing them. That's what we do. We are not a protest organization. We are actually doing law enforcement on the high seas. But since we're in international waters, there is no jurisdiction.

We are perceived as being radical extremists because we sink whaling ships and confiscate driftnets. What must be understood is that everything that we hit, attack, and sink is illegal. That's why after all of these years, sinking nine ships and causing multi-million of dollars worth of damage to our oppositions, we have never had a single criminal conviction. We are also proud to say we have never injured anyone or sustained an injury.

It is peculiar that if someone destroys something that is made by a human being—a work of art, architecture, whatever—our society calls that person a vandal. If someone destroys something that is a part of nature, or some would say, the work of God, we call them loggers, developers, and businessmen. It's just a question of values. We are raised in a culture that gives more value to material property than it does to living things.

Since everything is interconnected, every time you destroy a species, you diminish the integrity of the biosphere. The most important thing is to understand the law of ecology, biodiversity, interdependence, finite resources, and the law of species and precedents.

TASHA *Tudor*
& Rebecca and Owyn

"DON'T PEOPLE LOOK LIKE THEIR DOGS?"

I HAVE A ONE-TRACK MIND WHEN IT COMES TO CORGIS. I THINK IT IS BECAUSE THEY ARE Welsh, and my ancestors came from Wales. Don't people look like their dogs? Just like a man and wife who come to look like one another in a very happy marriage.

A prayer I like says, "God defend us from the Norsemen and their dogs." Corgis are herding dogs, working dogs. They do not herd sheep, rather cows and cattle. They are called "nippers" in Wales because they run behind the animals. The dogs squat down, which is why they have such short legs, so if a cow kicks, it goes over their heads and does not hit them. A well-trained Corgi is something to see.

I have had Corgis for about fifty years. My dogs come from the Swedish Valhund. It is claimed that they came over to England with the Flemish weavers in the 1500s. My younger son, Tom, fell in love with them when we lived in England. Both of my boys were deficient in Latin by the standards of English schools, so they had a tutor; the tutor had a Corgi, and Tom fell in love with it. Tom was determined to have a Corgi from Pembroke. He saved up his money and wrote to Reverend Jones in Wales. The vicar was so pleased that an American boy was interested in a Corgi that he picked out a perfectly beautiful one for him. He shipped the dog over in a tea chest on a Dutch airline. I still have the tea chest.

Gingersnap, 1997

Since English schools do not let out for the summer until July and the Corgi came to our home in May, I said to Tom, "You know he is going to bond with me and you will not be his master." Tom did not mind. It ended being absolutely true; he wanted nothing to do with Tom. That particular Corgi was a wonderful old boy.

JOHN PAUL *De Joria*
& Sammy, Donatello
and Herman

AT JOHN PAUL MITCHELL SYSTEMS, WE STRIVE TO PROTECT animals. Animals add life to the planet. We have never tested our products on animals at Paul Mitchell. We think it is very foolish to pick up a bunny and pour shampoo in the bunny's eye until it goes blind. We make products for human beings, not for animals, so we think it is only fair we test them on ourselves.

I think it is perfect to have Sammy here to represent the millions of bunnies we have saved. We support cruelty-free organizations like PETA. As a result of our support of these organizations, many larger or comparable-sized companies have followed our example and have stopped needless testing on animals.

You will never feel as good in your life as you do when you help an animal, and save its life, or save it from a miserable existence. The gratitude you receive is in knowing you did something to help a living being have a better life. That is good for all human beings.

DENISE *Brown*
SEAN & *Brown*
Tyson and Nicki

MY SON AND I EXPERIENCE PURE joy and love from Nicki and Tyson. I think that animals love unconditionally, something that I wish human beings could learn to do. Sadly I have learned, from domestic violence victims and their children who live in shelters, that the batterer often times abuses animal companions first. They injure the animals, or even kill them, to frighten and to threaten the victim. Unfortunately, since shelters do not take animals in with their families, many victims stay in abusive situations to protect the only thing that gives them love.

I think human beings who hurt helpless animals that trust and love them are pathetic. I have always thought that if adults could learn wisdom from children and animals, then we would all be better for that knowledge.

ALEXIS *Rockman*
&Celine and Kouros

A WHILE BACK, I HAD BEEN WORKING ON A body of work dealing with images that took place either inside farms or laboratories, places where organisms were put into a context where they were manipulated biologically or genetically. My primary concern was the breakdown of boundaries in terms of speciation—what defines a species. Animals may be altered beyond natural boundaries to the point of losing the characteristics of their own species. In laboratory and farm contexts, a lot of species have been manipulated by human particiption. It happens behind closed doors, where everything is done very secretively.

In these matters, we are kept on the outside by a wall of technology. Unless you understand the language, it is hard to know what is happening.

Biosphere Laboratory, 1993

I LEARNED MY LOVE FOR ANIMALS FROM MY MOTHER. It is not just love, but also respect, and kindness for the system of nature, and the importance of this system as knowledge for humanity.

While growing up in the country of the Ohio landscape, I was surrounded by creeks, woods, and cornfields. My mom always said we had a big red X marked on our door for the stray cats, dogs, baby owls, and an endless assortment of garter snakes and pet mice that lived with us. You can learn a lot about loving and caring by having animals around. It allows a perspective into another existence, even though that existence has been domesticated.

My relationship with Nika is one of love and trust. I rescued her five and a half years ago from the pound as a bowlegged pup, who could not be used for herding. Nika and I go everywhere together. She is one of my best friends and companions.

We all have a lot to learn about compassion, love, and respect. I think nature teaches us, if not making us more human, then more humane and wiser.

CATHERINE *Opie*
&Nika

ROY *Rogers* and DALE *Evans* & Charlie

YEARS AGO, WE HAD A DOG BY THE NAME OF Sam. He was very devoted to Roy. The strength of this devotion was demonstrated when Roy's heart problems forced him to be hospitalized. Sam was totally at a loss without him around.

Sam spent his days at our museum in Victorville. At the moment Roy went in for surgery, Sam lay down on a shelf in the museum's office . . . waiting. He stayed there for hours. When the operation was successfully completed, Sam stood up and walked away as if he had not a care in the world.

His vigil coincided exactly with the span of time Roy was on the operating table. His devotion never ceased to amaze us.

ELLIOTT *Erwitt* &Friends

"DOGS SEEM TO HAVE A NATURAL BOND WITH CHILDREN."

Dogs don't mind being photographed in compromising situations, but it is not that dogs are never self-conscious. In fact, a cruel person, or a photographer, can easily embarrass them. But they are usually unaffected because of their innocence, or lack of worldly experience. Perhaps that's why dogs seem to have a natural bond with children. Maybe they still have some fundamental values that haven't been corrupted by society.

Dogs are not exactly like children, though. They are more nonchalant. They don't necessarily want you to notice that they are around, because they know that they belong. Dogs don't have to say "Look at me!" the way your children often do.

Dogs have more to do than children. For one thing, they are forced to lead a life that is really schizoid. Every day, they have to live on two planes at once, juggling the dog world with the human world. And they're always on call. Their owners want instant affection every day, any time of day. A dog can never say that he has other things to do.

NYC, 1974

LINDA *Ellerbee* & **Beau**

I GAVE BEAU TO ROLFE, MY LIFE-PARTNER,

ten years ago. Everyday, Rolfe gives Beau back to me.

This way, we both get to love him and live with him.

Personally, I don't trust people who do not trust dogs.

TODD *Oldham*
& Mike and Betty

BETTY IS THIRTEEN AND MIKE is ten. They are my heroes and probably my greatest source of inspiration. They are the two beings with whom I like to spend the most time. Mike and Betty are very special to me.

PATRICK *McDonnell* & **Earl**

I HARDLY EVER THINK OF EARL AS MY "DOG." TO ME HE IS JUST EARL.

Comic strip, May 20, 1995

Sources

Actors and Others for Animals
11523 Burbank Blvd.
North Hollywood, CA 91601
(818) 755-6045
Fax: (818) 755-6048

A broad-based community organization working to end animal abuse. The organization focuses on the need for spaying and neutering and offers financial aid to the elderly, handicapped, and low-income families to have their pets altered.

Alliance for Animals
122 State St., Ste. 605
Madison, WI 53703-2500
(608) 257-6333
Fax: (608) 257-6400
E-mail: Alliance@AllAnimals.Org.

An organization devoted to increasing public awareness of animal abuse and promoting the humane treatment of all animals.

American Humane Association
63 Inverness Drive East
Englewood, CO 80112-5117
(800) 227-4645
(303) 792-9900
Fax: (303) 792-5333

This organization is a national leader in identifying and preventing the causes of animal abuse and neglect, and provides advocacy, training, research, technical assistance, and other services in the areas of child and animal protection.

American Society for the Prevention of Cruelty to Animals (ASPCA) NY
424 E. 92nd St.
New York, NY 10128
(212) 876-7700
Fax: (212) 410-7658
http://www.aspca.org

ASPCA, founded in 1866, was the first humane organization in the Western Hemisphere. Today, the ASPCA has over 400,000 members and continues to alleviate the pain, fear, and suffering of animals throughout nationwide education, awareness, and advocacy programs.

American Tortoise Rescue
5757 Wilshire Blvd., Ste. 165
Los Angeles, CA 90036-3686
(800) 938-3553
Fax: (213) 934-9910
E-mail: TurtleResQ@aol.com
http://www.tortoise.com

A nonprofit 501(c)(3) corporation founded in 1994 to provide for the rescue and rehabilitation of all species of tortoise and turtle.

Animal Legal Defense Fund
127 Fourth St.
Petaluma, CA 94952
(707) 769-7771
Fax: (707) 769-0785

A national nonprofit group of lawyers and law students who use their legal skills to protect animals.

Animal Legislative Action Network (ALAN)
2379 Panorama Terrace
Los Angeles, CA 90039
Phone and fax: (213) 662-6728

This is an animal-dedicated political action committee in the business of assuring the election of animal sensitive politicians, district attorneys, and judges.

Animal Protection Institute of America
P. O. Box 22505
Sacramento, CA 95822
(916) 731-5521 or (800) 348-7387
Fax: (916) 731-4467
http://www.g-net.com/api.htm
OnlineAPI@aol.com

This is a national animal advocacy nonprofit organization formed in 1968 dedicated to protecting animals against abuse through enforcement and legislative actions, investigations, advocacy campaigns, crisis intervention, public awareness, and education.

Animal Rescue Foundation of Dana Point (ARF)
P. O. Box 756
Dana Point, CA 92629
(714) 493-5251
Fax: (714) 493-5251, Dial 525

This organization is a nonprofit group of volunteers dedicated to the welfare and rescue of stray and lost animals in the city of Dana Point, CA.

Animal Rights International
P. O. Box 214
Planetarium Station
New York, NY 10024
(212) 873-3674

An organization that promotes a vegetarian lifestyle as well as the enhancement of public health, the liberation of animals, and the protection of our environment.

Animal's Agenda
P. O. Box 25881
Baltimore, MD 21224
(800) 426-6884
Fax: (703) 683-1523

This publication is the premier animal rights magazine in the United States. Articles and book reviews focus on animal rights and animal welfare issues, vegetarianism, and related political action topics.

Ark Trust, Inc.
5461 Noble Ave.
Van Nuys, CA 91411
(818) 786-9999
Fax: (818) 786-9070

A national, nonprofit animal protection organization that works proactively with the news and entertainment media to raise public awareness about the vast spectrum of animal issues. Each year, The Ark Trust presents the Genesis Awards, a star-studded, taped-for-television spectacular that honors individuals in the major media for handling animal issues with courage, creativity, and integrity.

British Union for the Abolition of Vivisection (BUAV)
16a Crane Grove
London, England N7 8LB
011-44-0171 700 4888
Fax: 011-44-0171 700 0252

Founded in 1898, the BUAV has been campaigning to end animal experiments for almost 100 years.

Dedication and Everlasting Love to Animals (DELTA) Rescue
P. O. Box 9
Glendale, CA 91209
(818) 241-6282
(805) 269-5049

Over 100 acres of no-kill, care-for-life animal shelters, housing over 1,000 dogs and cats with one thing in common: all were rescued from the wilderness by Leo Grillo. DELTA Rescue accepts no pets from the public, but instead, publishes a free book that includes information on placing unwanted pets.

Defenders of Wildlife
1101 Fourteenth St., Ste. 1400
Washington, DC 20005-5605
(202) 682-9400
Fax: (202) 682-1331
http://www.defenders.org

This organization protects wild animals and environments through education, litigation, research, and advocacy. It focuses especially on imperiled animals including wolves, bears, dolphins, tigers, wild birds, and elephants. At legacy can be made for these precious animals by naming Defenders in your will.

Dog's Home Battersea
4 Battersea Park Rd.
London, England SW8 4AA
Fax: 01-71-6226451

This organization rescues over 9,000 unwanted and stray dogs each year. It restores lost dogs to their owners and finds suitable homes for those that remain.

The Donkey Sanctuary
Sidmouth, Devon, England, EX10 0NU
011-44-1395-578222
Fax: 011-44-1395-579266
E-mail: 100731.3407@compuserve.com
http://www.vet.gla.ac.uk/inform/donkey/

Provides care, protection, and permanent security for donkeys in need of attention by reason of sickness, maltreatment, poor circumstances, ill-usage, or other causes as well as the prevention of cruelty and suffering among donkeys.

Doris Day Animal League
227 Massachusetts Ave., NE, Ste. 100
Washington, DC 20002-6084
(202) 546-1761
Fax: (202) 546-2193

An organization with an overriding mission to reduce the pain and suffering of animals and to increase the public's awareness of its responsibility toward animals through legislative initiatives, public education, and programs.

Farm Animal Reform Movement (FARM)
Post Office Box 30654
Bethesda, MD 20824
(301) 530-1737
Fax: (301) 530-5747
E-mail: farmusa@ecols.com
http://envirolink.org/arrs/farm

An organization that promotes planetary health through plant-based eating with natural grass-roots campaigns such as the Great American Meatout, World Farm Animals Day, and CHOICE (Consumers for Healthy Options in Children's Education).

Farm Animal Sanctuary
Post Office Cottage
Stoney Lane
Broad Green
Bromsgrove
Worcestershire B60 1LW, England
011-44-052778307

This sanctuary was created as Britain's first farm animal sanctuary to offer refuge to animals rescued from markets and farms.

Farm Sanctuary/East
P. O. Box 150
Watkins Glen, NY 14891
(607) 583-2225
Fax: (607) 583-2041, Holly
http://www.farmsanctuary.org

Farm Sanctuary/West
P.O. Box 1065
Orland, CA 95963
(916) 865-4617
Fax: (916) 865-4622

Farm Sanctuary has established the first shelters for victims of "food animal" production, successfully prosecuted stockyards and factory farms in precedent-setting cruelty cases, passed the first state law banning livestock marketing cruelties, and initiated ground-breaking investigative campaigns and national new exposés of the "food animal" industry.

Friends of Animals
1841 Broadway, Room 212
New York, NY 10023
(212) 247-8120
Fax: (212) 582-4482

An international, nonprofit membership organization working to protect animals from cruelty, abuse, and institutionalized exploitation.

Friends of the Sea Lion
Marine Mammal Center
20612 Laguna Canyon Rd.
Laguna Beach, CA 92651
(714) 494-3050
Fax: (714) 494-2802
http://www.tequen.com/fslmmc/

This nonprofit organization rescues, rehabilitates, and releases back to the wild sick and injured seals and sea lions along Orange County's coastline, with a rehabilitation rate among the highest in the state. Open daily to visitors.

Fund for Animals
200 W. 57th St.
New York, NY 10019
(212) 246-2016
Fax: (212) 246-2633
http://envirolink.org/arrs/fund

This organization is a national anti-cruelty society that works to relieve fear and suffering in all animals, wild and domestic. In addition to the Fund's work in pro-animal legislation, it also operates two low-cost spay/neuter clinics and vans, a wildlife rehabilitation center and a 1,000-acre refuge for abused hoofed animals, the Black Beauty Ranch, in Texas.

Jane Goodall Institute for Wildlife Research, Education and Conservation
P. O. Box 599
Ridgefield, CT 07866
(800) 999-CHIMP
(203) 431-2099
Fax: (203) 431-4387

This organization sponsors educational programs to increase awareness of wildlife and the environment and promotes initiatives to improve the well being of nonhuman primates in captivity. The Institute also supports re-forestation and sustainable land use projects throughout Africa and continues the uninterrupted research of wild chimpanzees in Tanzania's Gombe National Park.

Gorilla Foundation
Box 620-530
Woodside, CA 94062
(800) 63-GO APE
Fax: (415) 851-0291
http://www.gorilla.org.

An organization that works to promote awareness of the issues and threats that face free-living and captive gorillas and to promote and propagate this endangered species. The primary research focuses on long-term behavioral observation and an interspecies communication project with Koko and Michael, two western lowland gorillas.

Greenpeace
1436 U St., NW
Washington, DC 20009
(800) 784-4410
(202) 462-1177
Fax: (202) 462-4507
http://www.greanpeaceusa.org

An independent, campaigning organization which uses nonviolent, creative confrontation to expose global environmental problems, and to force the solutions which are essential to a green and peaceful future. Its goal is to ensure the ability of the earth to nurture life in all its diversity.

House Rabbit Society
1524 Benton St.
Alameda, CA 94501
(510) 521-4631
http://www.rabbit.org

A nonprofit rescue and education group dedicated to prolonging the quality of life for rabbits.

Humane Farming Association
1550 California St., Ste. 6
San Francisco, CA 94109
(415) 485-1495
Fax: (415) 485-0106

The nation's largest organization dedicated to the protection of farm animals. Over 100,000 members strong, HFA's comprehensive program includes: anti-cruelty investigations, direct hands-on emergency care and refuge for abused farm animals, national media and ad campaigns, legislation, legal action, and the highly successful National Veal Boycott and campaign against factory farming.

Humane Society of the United States (HSUS)
2100 L St., NW
Washington, DC 20037
(202) 452-1000 or (301) 258-3046
Fax: (202) 778-6132
http://www.hsus.org

This is the nation's largest animal-protection organization, with more than five million constituents. The HSUS was founded in 1954 to promote the humane treatment of animals, and to foster respect, understanding, and compassion for all creatures; today this message of care and protection embraces not only the animal kingdom, but also the earth and its environment.

International Fund for Animal Welfare (IFAW)
411 Main St.
Yarmouth Port, MA 02675-0193
(508) 362-6268
Fax: (508) 362-5841

Concerned with the Canadian seal hunt, anti-whaling, bear bile farms in China, fox hunting in the United Kingdom, African elephants, emergency relief, and pet rescue.

Jews for Animal Rights
255 Humphrey St.
Marblehead, MA 01945
Fax and Phone: (617) 639-0772
E-mail: micah@micahbooks.com
http://www.micahbooks.com

Micah Publications, the publishing arm of Jews for Animal Rights, publishes books on Judaism and vegetarianism, Judaism and animal rights, ritual material, and cookbooks for celebrating the Jewish holidays with vegetarian food.

Last Chance for Animals (LCA)
8033 Sunset Blvd., Ste. 35
Los Angeles, CA 90046
(800) 473-8843 or (310) 271-6096
Fax: (310) 271-1890

LCA obtains revealing video documentation of abuses against animals. It believes that media, and most specifically television, represents the best tool for educating people about issues that affect animals.

League Against Cruel Sports
Sparling House
83-87 Union St.
London, England SE1 15G
011-44-171-403- 6155
Fax: 011-44-171-403-4532
Email: 100647.3311@compuserve.com

The League Against Cruel Sports opposes hunting with dogs as it is cruel by design, inflicts unnecessary suffering, plays no part in the management of the animals hunted, and should not be tolerated in a civilized society.

The Marine Mammal Center
Marin Headlands
Golden Gate National Recreational Area
Sausalito, CA 94965
(415) 289-7325
Fax: (415) 289-7333

This organization rescues and rehabilitates hundreds of distressed marine mammals each year, and releases them back into the ocean when they are healthy. It also educates the thousands of adults and children who participate in its marine environmental programs at the shore, in classrooms, at its hospital site, and at its Interpretive Center.

National Anti-Vivisection Society (NAVS)
53 W. Jackson Blvd.
Chicago, IL 60604
(800) 888-NAVS
(800) 922-FROG Dissection Hotline
Fax: (312) 427-6524
E-mail: navs@navs.org
http://www.navs.org

Dedicated to abolishing the exploitation of animals used in research, education, and product testing. NAVS promotes greater compassion, respect, and justice for animals though educational programs based on respected ethical and scientific theory and supported by extensive documentation of the cruelty and waste of vivisection.

New England Anti-Vivisection Society (NEAVS)
333 Washington St., Ste. 850
Boston, MA 02108-5100
(617) 523-6020
Fax: (617) 523-7925
E-mail: info@ma.neavs.com
http://.www.neavs.org

NEAVS works to end animal experimentation (vivisection) through public outreach efforts, research, and publications. It sponsors educational programs designed to promote compassion and respect for animals, works with teachers and students to promote the use of alternatives to animals in the classroom, funds development of alternatives to the use of animals in product and cosmetic testing, and provides support and testimony on key animal protection bills.

Orange County People for Animals (OCPA)
Box 14187
Irvine, CA 92623-4187
(714) 751-OCPA (6272) for a recorded message
of animal rights news in area
Fax: (714) 955-3553

OCPA is Orange County's largest, oldest, and most active animal rights group, founded in 1988 by Ava Park. It promotes the concept of "rights for all living beings," and militant nonviolence in the tradition of Gandhi. Its activities include public demonstrations on issues of vivisection, fur, factory farming, and animals in entertainment.

Pets Are Wonderful Support For People Living With HIV/AIDS (PAWS)/LA
7327 Santa Monica Blvd.
North Hollywood, CA 90046
(213) 876-7297
Fax: (213) 876-0511

PAWS/LA is a non-profit organization founded in 1989 to serve the greater Los Angeles area. It is dedicated to brightening and easing the lives of people living with HIV/AIDS and their pets by providing compassionate assistance with the care and feeding of their animals.

Performing Animal Welfare Society (PAWS)
P. O. Box 849
Galt, CA 95632
(209) 745-2606
Fax: (209) 745-1809

This organization is dedicated to rescuing exotic and performing animals from cruel confinement and pain. Abandoned or abused performing animals and victims of the exotic animal trade can live at the sanctuary in peace and contentment. It also educates the general public, veterinarians, and the entertainment industry about inhumane animal training and treatment and tries to strengthen laws on animals' behalf.

People for the Ethical Treatment of Animals (PETA)
501 Front St.
Norfolk, VA 23510
(757) 622-PETA
Fax: (757) 622-1273

PETA is an international nonprofit animal protection organization dedicated to establishing and defending the rights of all animals. With more than 500,000 members worldwide, PETA works through public education, research and investigations, legislation, special events, direct action, and grassroots organizing.

Physician's Committee for Responsible Medicine
5100 Wisconsin Ave., Ste. 404
Washington, DC 20016
(202) 686-2210
Fax: (202) 686-2216

A nonprofit organization dedicated to advocating the health benefits of a vegan diet and promoting alternatives to animal research.

Sea Shepherd Conservation Society
P. O. Box 628
Venice, CA 90294
(310) 301-SEAL (7325)
Fax: (310) 574-3161

International law applies on the high seas, but modern-day pirates have been free to loot the living treasures of the ocean because there is little will on the part of nations to enforce those laws. In response, Paul Watson founded the Sea Shepherd Conservation Society in 1977. It is the only official organization that actively defends the oceans of the world from rampant exploitation, preserving marine ecosystems and wildlife for future generations.

Sentient Creatures, Inc.
P. O. Box 765
Cathedral Station
New York, NY 10025
(212) 865-5998

This is a tax-exempt, non-profit grassroots organization renowned for its 23 years of service to rescuing, rehabilitating, and placing over 2,000 junkyard cats and dogs from Harlem, New York City, into loving homes.

Society for Prevention of Cruelty to Animals Los Angeles (spcaLA)
5026 W. Jefferson Blvd.
Los Angeles, CA 90016
(213) 730-5300
Fax: (213) 730-5333

This is a nonprofit animal welfare organization dedicated to the welfare of all animals. Founded in 1877, spcaLA was originally chartered to end the abuse of horses used in travel, then expanded to include child and pet abuse cases. Its programs and services today include Investigation and Rescue, Humane Education, Disaster Response, sheltering homeless and abused animals, and adopting spayed or neutered pets.

United Poultry Concerns, Inc.
P. O. Box 59367
Potomac, MD 20859
Phone and fax: (301) 948-2406
http://www.envirolink.org/arrs/upc

A nonprofit organization that addresses the treatment of domestic fowl in food production, science, education, entertainment, and human companionship situations. It promotes the compassionate and respectful treatment of domestic fowl. Karen Davis, PhD, president, is the author of *Prisoned Chickens, Poisoned Eggs: An Inside Look at the Modern Poultry Industry* (The Book Publishing Company, 1996).

Wildlife Rescue and Rehabilitation, Inc.
P. O. Box 34FF
San Antonio, TX 78201
(210) 698-1709
Fax: (210) 698-1710

This organization rescues, rehabilitates, and releases injured, orphaned, and abused wild animals. It also provides permanent and natural enclosures for nonreleasable indigenous and nonindigenous wildlife.

Wildlife Waystation
14831 Little Tujunga Canyon Road
Angeles National Forest, CA 91342-5999
(818) 899-5201
Fax: (818) 890-1107
http://www.waystation.org

This is a nonprofit charitable facility which cares for abandoned, injured, and abused wildlife. It is home to more than 1,000 permanent residents and a rehabilitation center for another 4,000 animals a year. Tours available, by reservation, the first and third Sundays of every month.

World Society for the Protection of Animals
29 Perkins St.
P. O. Box 190
Boston, MA 02130
(800) 883-WSPA
Fax: (617) 522-7077

An international animal protection organization dedicated to helping all species of animals. Issues include humane stray control, anti-bullfighting, animal rescue, wildlife rehabilitation, and release.

World Wildlife Fund
1250 Twenty-Fourth St., NW
Washington, DC 20037
(202) 293-4800
Fax: (202) 293-9211

WWF, known worldwide by its panda logo, leads international efforts to save life on earth. Now in its fourth decade, WWF works in more than 100 countries around the globe. It is a conservation organization working to protect endangered species.

Credits

22: Copyright © Jamie Wyeth: Kleberg, 1984.
Oil on canvas,
30 1/2" x 42 1/2"

30: Wyland: Leap of Faith (Whaling Wall 57), Seattle, WA, 1994.
Copyright © Wyland Studios, 30' x 50'

38: Beatrice Wood: Untitled, 1996.
Colored pencil,
9" x 12"

54: Audrey Flack: Bounty, 1978.
Oil and acrylic on canvas,
80 1/4" x 67 1/4"
Reynolda House, Museum of American Art, Winston-Salem, North Carolina

64: R.C. Gorman: Honky, 1995; Lola, 1995.
Ceramic plates,
12" x 14 1/2"

70: Sue Coe: They Made Themselves Extinct, 1997.
Lithograph, 15" x 20"
Copyright © Sue Coe

78: Judy Chicago: Would You Wear Your Dog?
Polaroid Transfer and Gouache on Rag Paper,
15" x 22"
Copyright © Judy Chicago, 1992 with Photography © by Donald Woodman

82: Seldes, George. *Great Thoughts. The Future of Man by Victor Hugo*, p.194. New York: Ballantine Books, 1985.

84: Dratfield, Jim and Paul Couglin. *The Quotable Feline.* New York: Alfred A. Knopf, 1996.

88: William Wegman: Untitled, 1994.
Unique Polacolor ER Print,
20" x 24"
© William Wegman
Courtesy of PaceWildensteinMacGill, NY

90: Walker, G.F. *Medical World*, p. 365. 1933.

96: Alexandra Day: Illustration from *Carl's Birthday.*
Copyright © 1995 by Alexandra Day. Reprinted by permission of Farrar, Straus & Giroux, Inc.

102: Robert Rauschenberg: Prego (Urban Bourbon Series), 1991.
Acrylic on enameled aluminum,
49" x 37"

110: Matuschka: Alabama Dog, 1989.
Black and white photograph
Copyright © Matuschka

122: Rachel Rosenthal: Tatti Exploring My Shoulder After I Shaved My Head, 1996.
Pen and Ink,
8 1/2" x 11"

136: Tasha Tudor: Gingersnap, 1997.
Pastel,
9" x 12"
Gingersnap Copyright © 1997 Corgi Cottage Industries, L.L.C.

142: Alexis Rockman: Biosphere Laboratory, 1993.
Oil on two wood panels,
96" x 128"
Courtesy Jay Gorney Modern Art, NY

148: Elliott Erwitt: NYC, 1974.
Black and white photograph
© Elliott Erwitt
Excerpted from the book *To The Dogs* by Elliott Erwit
Copyright © 1992 D.A.P, Scalo

154: Patrick McDonnell: *Mutts*, Comic strip, May 20, 1995.
Reprinted with permission of King Features Syndicate

Cleveland Amory 🐕 Sonny Barger 🐕 De

🐕 Judy Chicago 🐈 Sue Coe 🐕 Judy Col

Marc Davis 🐕 Alexandra Day 🐕 John

Richard Donner 🐕 Danny Elfman 🐕 David

🐕 Shera Danese Falk 🐕 Audrey Flack 🐕 M

Ph.D., CBE 🐕 R.C. Gorman 🐕 Elliott Gould

🐕 Engelbert Humperdinck 🐕 Beverly Johns

🐕 Vicki Lawrence 🐈 Greg Louganis 🐕

Patrick McDonnell 🐕 Matuschka 🐕 Burg

Navratilova 🐕 Kevin Nealon 🐕 Ingrid New

Alex Pacheco 🐕 Robert Pastorelli 🐕 M

Rauschenberg 🐈 Alexis Rockman 🐕 Mor

and Dale Evans 🐕 Mickey Rooney 🐕 Ra

Grace Slick 🐕 Barbara Bach Starkey 🐕

Thompson 🐕 Tasha Tudor 🐕 Peter Vidr

William Wegman 🐕 Beatrice Wood 🐕 Jan